73

Birthday Girl with Possum
a collection of poetry

☙

by Brendan Constantine

WRITEBLOODY
QUALITY AMERICAN BOOKS

Write Bloody Publishing
America's Independent Press

Long Beach, CA

WRITEBLOODY.COM

For Mindy
With every
Good Wish!

[signature]

Constantine, Brendan.
1ˢᵗ edition.
ISBN: 978-1-935904-36-6

Interior Layout by Lea C. Deschenes
Cover Designed by Bill Jonas
Proofread by Jennifer Roach and Sarah Kay
Edited by Jamie Garbacik, Courtney Olsen, Alexis Davis, Sarah Kay, and Derrick Brown
Type set in Bergamo from www.theleagueofmoveabletype.com

Special thanks to Lightning Bolt Donor, Weston Renoud

Printed in Tennessee, USA

Write Bloody Publishing
Long Beach, CA
Support Independent Presses
writebloody.com

To contact the author, send an email to writebloody@gmail.com

For my mother & father

Birthday Girl with Possum

BIRTHDAY GIRL (WITH POSSUM)

PART I
The House of the World

PART II
Crimewave

PART III
Hyenas in the Temples
of Pleasure

The Favor of Your Company

There would be no sand,
    there would be no sea,

no straw, no bird, no tree
    in a window, no window

There would be no shadow,
    there would be no lamp,

no word, no letter, no stamp
    from France, no France,

no feast, no reason to dance,
    for no reason at all

had a coat not hung on a wall,
    had not a cup been spilled

& laughed about
              & filled

PART I

THE HOUSE
OF THE
WORLD

"The mad one is gone, leaving the house of the world in my charge and keeping. It is a ruined house, left from fool to fool."
                                        —Bektashi folklore

Noct

I was com
      You said you would wai

Twelve hundred miles in a day—
I counted houses, then their ligh

Came home to an empt
Not even my shir
      my green shir

Are you wearing it now?

It's hot, the house is hot; the walls,
even the handle on the refr

What the f
    What can anyone hope to keep?

If either of us could answer,
wou

1981

I learned the word disaster meant against the stars,
learned it did not apply to this world; the sky intended
every cruelty.
        I watched the boy with no legs draw
pictures of feet for an hour in Study Hall.
                In the hall
of my uncle's rest home I heard the paper voice of a man
so old he'd forgotten he was blind. When a nurse passed
his door, he'd ask "Turn the lights on, would you?"

I learned sadness like a way home from school. I got in
later and later. Some nights I didn't come back at all
but sat up waiting for myself.
            I passed Geography,
History, & Spanish for the last time. My cat died.
My dog turned grey. My physics teacher was hit
by an ambulance.
            But I read a book & understood it.
A woman asked me to touch her body. I did.
                I wrote
my first poem. It said people were like moons. I believed
what I wrote, believed I had done all my writing, wouldn't
do anymore.
            Then I believed a book that said the oleanders
behind our house were poison. All summer I dreamed
of meeting someone I could feed one brutal flower.

THE MANAGER

My daughters learned to sing
in your bathroom. The acoustics
made them feel famous. Their father
died cleaning your carpet, though I
suspect it was the strain of carrying
your sink up three flights that did it.
I mourned him & finished the rug.
My daughters have daughters & they
pass your door when they visit.
They wonder if you're nice. I say
I don't know; simpler than asking
why it matters. Just as each time
someone leaves me, the landlord
doesn't apologize. He offers me
something smaller & I accept.
It's how I manage. I make room.

POEM ENDING ON A LINE
BY THE DEPARTMENT OF WATER AND POWER

Someone is always playing a drum.
The birds are each a different color
and the volcano is new. We call this
the spare bedroom.

Will you be staying long, or don't
you know yet? You shouldn't
have any trouble getting to sleep.
The bed is as soft as the earth.

Please take a moment to fill out
the questionnaire on your pillow.
My name is Encyclopedia. If you need
books or extra blankets, look me up.

There is a tropical storm scheduled
for this evening. The rain will taste
of mangoes. If you disagree with water
and electrical charges, please call.

L O O K at the / look at / look at you
you've got the whole / it's like we all /
just look at you / Surprise the curtains /
the car / the lawn and the old / the river
came right to your door. You stepped /
some mornings / and leaf / well you'd
be / swear the whole forest looked into
you / There was a bird / those birds / a
yellow one with / it had a blackness to /
you said it was imitating the electricity
in all the / pretty / though / so / clear /
a lark with a crystal throat / care / -ful /
sound / sounded / so / you / Hh! / You

GEEK LOVE

If I had your action figure, I'd put your whole head
in my mouth; walk around that way, your legs stuck
out, arms hanging down, little gun or sword lost
in my crushed carpet. I'd make people deal with it—
clerks, waiters, people in elevators—drive friends
crazy over the phone with my slurping. I'd suck
on your head & suck on it until the paint cracked,
your eyes, mouth, & hair wore away, like the vow
on a candy Valentine. There'd be no stopping, then.
How could I let anyone see, who might remember
you brand new, so collectible in your vintage box.

If I had your action figure, I'd make you beat up all
my other action figures; I'd give you their secrets,
their weapons & armor, while they watched. Each
would be given a choice of fates: to be torn apart
by a giant baby or exile to a quiet Lego village
on a lake of glass. When they didn't answer,
I'd say I lied about the village.

If I had your action figure, I'd pose you & pose you
until it felt like you were really moving, working
against my hand, saying with your body, *This is how
I look when I run, how I look when I fly, & this—
hold up your arms—this is how I look
when I block out the sun.*

THE TRANSLATION

I once loved a girl with Russian Flu.
Every day I climbed her tree house,
to sit at her side and read Chekhov
in search of a cure. Neither of us
knew what the strange words meant
or if I said them right, but she would
sometimes nod weakly, her forehead
damp with candlelight, and say Now
we're getting somewhere, though we
never did before she slept. How many
nights did I climb down fearing
my pronunciation kept her ill?
How many branches hold the heart
above the belly? What noisy book is read
in the house of the heart, fruitlessly?
One morning I woke to snow, the entire
forest revised. When I got to her, she
had passed completely from translation,
even her name no longer the right word
for her. I spoke it anyway, over and again
until it sounded wrong to me, spoke it
back into noise, then left it in the woods
for storms to say.

The Oracle

A man in the UK changed his name
to They,   so he can say he says
what They say

If you stroke an alligator, sleep
in paper gloves, burn candles
while you're out, or swim after
thinking about wine

you'll come into money, stay young,
put the beast to sleep, drown
& burn down,
                    They *says*

Yeah, you've got to want it
                              Red skies
at morning, a crossed crack, white
dogs singing to a siren at night
might mean rain, but what doesn't

His ID is in the mail; no talking
They out of it now. Let's hope
he goes all the way:

Name: They
        Home: Yonder
                Age: The hills

THE SHAPES OF OUR BODIES IN SLEEP

You're usually running away,
the letter S in full stride, holding
the pillow to your ear as if listening
where to turn.
               I'm either the letter K,
chasing you, walking home, or H,
dancing exaltations to gods of sleep;
arms raised, chest thrust out, legs
bowed with a weight of music.

Sometimes you're dancing, too,
but a different dance, older than letters;
head down, a pinch of gown in each
hand, feet crossed to spin or bow
goodnight.
              Last night I was a dead sailor
spread like an X, waiting for a cop
to roll me over, to draw my outline.
You made a break for the harbor.

As Agreed

You get the right
side of the sea
I get my pick
of the bones

You get first peak
on Volcano Day
I get last dance

You reserve
all legal right
I get the left
side of the sea

The smoke we divide

You call dibs
on the organs
I choose the music

You get the harp
I get the picture
of the harp

You the phone
Me the door

You the wall
Me the creak

You numbers
Me teeth
No, me numbers
You teeth

You cactus
Me matches

You mermaid lamp
Me box spring

You consonants
Me vowels

You continents
Me condiments

and the sugar
we reckon like smoke

THE THINGS

The things I gave you—Victorian postcards,
a wind-up bird, the marzipan skull from Mexico
—don't recognize me

When I come to visit, Buddha slouches
in his ashtray, the wind mobile chimes
among itself
               What have you told them

In my room, your picture looks me in the eye;
I don't know who it's seeing

The things you gave me—a cup, a compass,
the tiniest flashlight—are all about going
What do I tell them

Even now, your music waits in the car

THE GATHERER

It's true, people take things
but rarely. A crash-site is
sacred, we're faithful. Rings,
watches, money; that stuff
never winds up in a pocket,
honest. It's your pictures
we have a hard time turning
over. At least half of you
bring them, to or from where-
ever. Think of it; we find you
in trees or pieced out across
a field, then match you up to
a burned or muddy carry-on
& there you are, smiling back
from a passport, a mountain,
a tideless beach, at silly us
making such a fuss. Only
once have I kept anything,
but it didn't belong to you,
not really. It's a picture
I took myself, my first time
on a sift. The event was
major, a three mile scatter,
no survivors. I had a camera
& instructions not to touch,
just record what there was
of you. It was a left hand—
a young man's, broken off
clean as fruit—two fingers
crossed. I made duplicates,
filed one, framed the other,
though it has never hung. I
keep it in a suitcase. It flies
when I fly.

Taking a Plane to Bed

we undress / take our usual
positions / me on the right /

you by the lamp & clock /
the plane is small / shrunk /
about the length of the bed /

there's no one onboard /
we each take a wing / pull
to our chins / the belly —

it's mostly belly— warm
between us / we can't draw
the sheets / don't need them /

I turn / throw a leg over
the tail / look thru the side/
you're already descending /

your eye in the window /
a hurricane bay /all the trees
blown down

PART II

CRIMEWAVE

"Each soul is a little grain of rice, lord of everything whatsoever there is."
—Brihad-aranyaka Upanishad

"I have too great a soul to die like a criminal."
—John Wilkes Booth

ALIBI & GOODNIGHT

I didn't see nothing. The rules was
broke when I got here. What happened is
the sun boiled over the rim,

    got on everything. Everybody starts
pointing & the cops arrive, like maybe
somebody thought the cops should arrive.

    I seen cops before in books, so I skipped
out the back. The sun was waiting, hit
me full in the face. When I came to

    it was all over the radio: night *fell*
or was pushed.

Lecture On Thomas Edison

In 1887 Thomas Edison began electrocuting dogs
for the press. He called it his duty to warn us
against the "evil" of Alternating Current,
a power he failed to discover first.
                                        It was not killing,
he told a reporter, the dogs had been
Westinghoused.
                        When he was twelve, Edison lost half
his hearing. No one knew how, but there were many
theories; one that he was pulled aboard a train
by his ears. Another, that he repeatedly forced coins
into them to attract lightning.
                                        There were cats, too,
& birds when he could get the electrodes to fit. Once,
he even wired a sunflower which opened like an eye
to weep out its seeds.
                        From his crib, Edison
routinely blew out his bedside candles, howling until
they were relit. On several mornings, his mother
woke to find a half-eaten stub dried to the infant's
gown.
        In 1903 he ran 6,600 Volts through an elephant
named Topsy. She had killed three men, the last a drunk
who gave her a cigarette. Edison filmed her execution
to play for whomever might ask.
                                        Upon hearing
his own voice through a phonograph, he exclaimed *I am
always afraid of things that work the first time.*

THE STRAY BULLETS OF LOS ANGELES

come out at night / come out at morning /
they have no jungle hour / no rest / lest
they're chambered / loaded into stalls
for slaughter / this morning two flew
in front of my car / just missed / well
forget finding them after / their master /
their muzzle / what then / they're wild /
all of a sudden / my sister had one come
through her back door / never found it /
probably hiding in a wall / they say
most homes have them now / under
the paint / holes / furrows / they burrow
& nest / but they came before the houses
came / before the road / led us thus /
scouts / going off / ahead of the wagons

A Little Black

The children of Juarez have run out
of red crayons. There's so much blood

in their eyes; the bodies of mules
dumped in their schools, hands & heads

by the road, blood in pools, blood
in stories of blood. Before I know it,

I'm planning my own crime, the worst
a poet can commit: to steal suffering,

call it mine. How vivid, I think, what
a strong detail on which to build.

I open my computer, the great self-
making book of our age, search for

more of the story, for the words *run
out of red crayons*. I find children

out of red in Pakistan, in Haiti, no red
left in Afghanistan, none in Georgia.

The children of Sierra Leon have gone
through pink to purple, in Myanmar

they're down to brown. I thought I had
something to add. I have nothing to add

but a little black, the color of the line,
color that consumes all others.

LECTURE ON SIGMUND FREUD

Sigmund Freud is the Mother of Modern Psychology.
The father has not been identified; Freud never revealed
his name. However, it's a fact that Freud bore him
hundreds of children.

The first was a boy named Oedipus Complex: S. Freud

> *I found in myself a constant love*
> *for my mother and jealousy*
> *of my father. I now consider this*
> *to be a universal event...*

Though many in the field denied wanting Freud's mother,
the public embraced the concept as easy to read.

Freud's other children of note include Genitalia, Headaches,
Babies & The Unconscious Mind, though he denied this last,
explaining that the child was merely left at his door.

The Unconscious Mind failed to identify Freud's picture
during repeated depositions.

In later life, Freud began to age. Unable to cope with menopause
& public demand for new children, he had his jaw replaced
with a plastic one.

It wasn't enough; in the fall of 1939
Sigmund Freud died of exposure.

Q: Do men and women want the same things?

A: There is no single fetal position.

THE AGENT

It isn't like smoking a cigarette
to make the bus come, sleeping
so the phone will ring; chance is
a holy covenant, destiny a card
on your windshield. I insure
disaster. *Earthquake* means
you've bought a fire, because
if the earth quakes enough, fire
comes & you aren't covered.
Fire buys you a flood. Men
in my business say if anyone
sells you a Love policy, take'em
down, but don't leave a mark
he can photograph. The grief
of our art is we didn't foresee
cameras. I once had a claim
where the client sent pictures
of a tornado that carried off
his family; one of the storm
coming, another as it passed
through the nursery. To me
it was a mug shot of God.

THE INQUISITION

I know a vegetarian who won't
give his money to the homeless because
he says they'll only use it to buy meat.
I know a junkie who says she just wants
to smoke crack like a normal person does.
For my part I would like to cross the street
without a rush of guilt for my dead cat,
my gentle hostage who ran from her name.
But how the hell are we supposed to live
with mercy when judgment is exquisite;
find us a better drug than laying blame.
I know a little girl who has to give
one punishment a day to all her toys.
She hates it, but they don't give her a choice.

LECTURE ON ALBERT EINSTEIN

Einstein was born in 1879, which is already pretty
brilliant.
    Most people couldn't drive or tell you where
the lights were but when his mom brought home a baby
sister, he knew to ask,
       Where are her wheels?
            My big
red dictionary defines time as a period, then later
as *an interval.*
      Granted, it's the 1920 edition—love
is defined as *a losing score in tennis*, the Giant Panda
as *the opposite of Lesser Panda*—but in 1921 Einstein
won the Nobel.
      All America did was smile at Europe
& then invent the Vibraphone.
         It's still embarrassing,
though it helps to pretend Time & Space are just ideas,
like islands or maps.
       When Einstein asked a conductor,
What time does Oxford stop at this train, he meant
every moment of it.
       He meant, *Look out the window
& tell me the wheels aren't turning the earth. Tell me
God plays dice. Tell me the force of a kiss will put
any body at rest.*
      In 1955 all the blood left his heart,
& ran to his feet, though no one knows when it arrived;
news out of Jersey has always been sketchy.
            However
I can tell you, for poetry makes nothingness happen,
that's-when-time-slowed-down-to-the-present
crawl.
    Before the year was out, Emmett Till was put
to death under the law of inertia.
        Everyone was singing
Ain't That a Shame.

You, Shouting

for Sarah Maclay

The roots of your face, how surprised we are
to see them. The parlor door behind you,
closed because we are not invited there,
how it opens an inch on its own. We can
just make out the piano. How it looks
like a cow back there. How you swallow
the door shut again. The chandelier,
its verdigris bouquet of flowers, how
it sways with you. How the few shadows
of this hour catch in the leaves, the bent
leaves, the leaves that must have bent
the last time it was taken down, the last time
it was held.

THE LIAR, THE CHEAT, & THE THIEF

Trust me, I'd lie to you
if I could.   If I could
think of a lie the size of night
I'd prove the world wasn't
made for the dead,
but it was.   It was
because the cat was never
more worldly than when it lay
in the road.
              No sooner
had I stopped, than a cop
appeared; drawn from his
speed trap. I said I might've
hit an animal, but couldn't
find it. He cast his heavy light
on the tarmac, got an answer
from a jeweled collar. *Oh yeah,*
he said, Yeah, you did.
                    Black,
small as a hat, the cat lay curled
into itself as though dozing off
a bird.   A bird
called from a phone-pole to say
we'd woken it. The cop said
You better get out of here;
I'll take care of this. At first
I didn't know whom he meant

and then I didn't know how
he meant it. Would he look
for a name tag, make the drive,
break the news? Or would he
keep the collar, move the body,
frame a stray dog for the crime?
He watched me get in my car,
watched me make a show
of going.

I tell you, if I hadn't
felt his eye all the way to you,
I might have driven until I found
another cat, might have gotten
out and walked the forty years
home. I tell you, I might have lain
down in the god-niverous dark.

LECTURE ON EMMETT TILL
(poem ending on a line from Scientific American)

The measure of disorder is
called Entropy. It marks the difference between
the past & future, giving direction to time:
Emmett Till winks or waves or speaks
or says nothing to Carolyn Bryant.
                                        She begins
to accelerate. The smaller body, Emmett Till
is thus caught in her orbit. As she runs to her car,
Till is spun home. The resulting vacuum fills
with talk–the entropy of smiling or not, waving
or not, saying "Bye, Baby"
                                        or eating candy.
Greater vacuums appear; the star of Mississippi
goes nova, then collapses, becoming a hole
in space. Its edge is an Event Horizon, a ring
of inert men from whom even light cannot
escape.
         The point at which Emmett Till enters
this region is not known. The best calculations
put it at midnight, 100 hours from eclipsing
the woman. Upon entering, he is drawn to
a singularity of infinite density,
                                        a dynamic
known as Teaching A Boy A Lesson.
Afterwards little of him is recognizable. He is
returned to the earth as mass or energy, "rock
of waters," the meaning of the word Tallahatchie,
the river where he reappears.
                                        His remains
are highly charged, continuously re-nucleating,
expanding with each revelation. Some studies
imply the belt of men has dispersed. Other math
suggests replacement by new bodies.
                                        Radical data
indicate stasis, polarized values, forced harmony.
Under this stress, some develop a halo.

SOMETHING YOU CAN USE

"Sunt lacrimae rerum et mentem mortalia tangunt "
These are the tears of things & to touch the thought of them is fatal.
—Vergil , The Aeneid

There are 14 shopping days until Christmas
so I have driven to the coroner's office.
They have a gift shop. There's no sign
that says GIFT SHOP UPSTAIRS—MORGUE
DOWN, you gotta' ask for it. You have to buzz
a gray man who opens the heavy green
door & looks at you like he's already tired
of your questions. I say, *Gifts?* He says
Take the elevator.
        It's on the second floor,
down an unlit hall, in what might have been
the mail room or a bird house; the walls
are cubbied. I need to find something
for my folks. Dad says I have a morbid sense
of humor. What I have is faith in the smile
on a naked skull. I smoke five cigarettes
a night.
        Somehow there aren't any ashtrays
for sale, but there are printed hats & T-shirts,
toe-tag key chains, garment bags made to look
like body bags. For mom, I choose a red blouse
with LA County Coroner in glittery cursive,
for dad, a black bath towel embroidered
with the white outline of a body.
        The girl
at the counter tells me sales have tripled
& they don't even advertise. She has an easy
smile that makes me feel like I'm her friend
or even her brother who remembers the day
she interviewed & neither of us thought
the place would stay in business,
but now look at it.

Walking away, I notice
another building, one I'd somehow missed
coming in. It looks more like a lost house,
standing awkwardly at the edge of the lot, as if
no one knew where to put it. There's a hand-
painted sign that reads *Thrift Shop* & it means
what I think it means. The girl at this counter
has no smile. Her face says she's never sold
anything to anyone.

        She's here because some-
body has to be, because things keep coming in
from next door, because the dead always come
wrapped. It's all priced to move: men's suits,
$10; sweaters, $2; shirts, $1.50. There are tables
of shoes, crowded like fish-market crabs, mostly
black, but here & there are flashes of light; a pair
of silver sling-backs,

        red cha-chas, like new.
On the floor, boxes of infants' wear. Someone
maybe this girl, has topped them with bibs, each
adorned with a baby jungle animal; a giraffe in two
pairs of pants, a tiger cub with a fireman's hat,
a monkey asleep in a coconut tree.

SCHOOL OF ECHOES
for a boy named Jack

Everything's said three times, written
three times in chalk, heard & heard

Third time's the charm of the country,
the canyon, the cave-painted herd

stampeded into firelight

Classes begin with *Goodbye*, end on
Hello   Between, it's mostly *Yodelay-*

heehoo   There isn't much home-
work: you read from your diary

in an underground parking lot,

fire a gun in church, or lie to a child
For extra credit you might raise

peacocks, memorize recordings
of dogs barking out their days

of barking out their days

Valedictorian gets lost at sea,
& cries, *Ahoy there, Ahoy please…*

The teachers do little but listen
& throb in their shoes like trees

The final exam's a breeze

LECTURE ON THE HUMAN BRAIN

The Brain is divided into two distinct hemispheres:
The Left Brain & Downtown.

The Left Brain processes experience linearly.
Downtown interprets the world as a single event.

The Left Brain understands itself as a chain of ideas
while Downtown knows itself to be all there is.

Hence, the former is always wrong while the latter
doesn't care. Both regions are joined

by the Corpus Callosum, & therefore are not so much
halves as alternate ends of the same third thing;

Suffix & Prefix to a Narthex Sublime.

The stem of the brain is called The Brain Stem
(or Stem). By this axis the brain may be plucked
& brought home.

Q: Is there a right side of the brain?

A: No. This is why Superman costumes are packaged
   with warnings.

THE PLAYER

What you don't hurt
can't know you. God
made our teeth white
to catch sun, to be
seen in dusk. Find me
a striped suit that isn't
zebra. Blood & money
smell the same. So do
fear & ink. No amount
of study is equal to
a quiet step. Let dust
into your eye, the fly
land on your cheek.
If you are still enough
the world will feed
itself to you. Wear one
color, have one sound,
step into the limousine
like a river.

"So God Will Know You"

After Miroslav Valek

Go out, get us some money
and kill a dog. Take this coat,
this book of matches, a knife
from the wall to kill a dog
on the way. You need medicine;
if not now, you will – aspirin,
quinine, a packet of God.
These things are still strong
enough to heal the country
and kill a dog. Sulfur traps
in their intestines, from fruit,
toad stools; any limb off
a chocolate rabbit is death,
as it happens. This happens:
we spread a newspaper, cut
an onion, wait with each other.
You kill a dog; a shepherd, a bull,
a fool hound. Tell whoever
complains the dog has killed
your dog first, your older dog.
They won't persist. The earth
is fed on the incorrigible. People
here worship this about the land;
that it is made rich by eating
thieves: the rabbit, the crow,
the pale gopher. Thus and so
we light a fire in a fireplace
and read half our book. Or sleep
in our beds and wake standing
by the window. If we call out,
the dogs inside us run away,
then creep back. They can
never come under our hands,
their softnesses. You must
keep the right things with you,

the family spoons, good spoons
to trade, to dig, to attract a dog.
You must expect to lose these
or not get enough for them. Have
some tea or ginger in your pocket
to offer the hermit, the widow
who takes you in against night,
the wild boy-man who thinks
he must be alone. Have a way
to mention us so they know
you cannot linger. At dawn
come home with money;
on the way, kill a dog.

LECTURE ON THE COUNTRY OF AMERICA

The tiny country of America is the smallest in the world.
Its primary export is language, describing two thirds
of its economy. The chief currency is the stammer.

Annual rainfall is unpronounceable.

The country was originally found by Chief Powhatan
of the Algonquin Nation.

I woke as the land was rising
it asked what I dreamed
I answered running

Contractors arrived in 1607, but development stalled
while land rights were sought from each tribe.

The sale of America was ultimately ratified by families
listening to radio on August 6th, 1945. Today the country
is home to hundreds & may one day join the UN.

The National Flower has not emerged.

Q: How much does America weigh?

A: About the same as the slave ship *Clotilda*, minus payload.

PRE-LANDING CHECKLIST
for Nicole Harvey

14. no one is actually talking
    to you, except to say this

13. all food is wild

12. someone has got to die

11. if you're not rock, paper,
    or scissors, you're the back
    of the horse

10. you're asleep for most of it

9. you're on stage only briefly

8. if you want to play Ophelia,
   you've got to get wet

7. it's too soon to think about
   survivors

6. everyone already ate, several
   times, & they're not done

5. they never just want Poland

4. killers expect to be filmed

3. film adds exactly ten years

2. it's all day & into the night
   & all day

1. the people, all of them, are
   the actual people

PART III

HYENAS
IN THE TEMPLES
OF PLEASURE

"...Wild beasts shall lie there, and owls shall call there, and satres shall dance there and hyenas shall cry in the temples of pleasure."
— Isaiah 13:21 - 22

FALL MEMO
Please be aware of the following students and their sensitivities

Miranda R.	peanuts, common wheat
Lucas P.	dogs, strawberries
Kimmy D.	aspirin, penicillin, rhubarb
Alexis M.	trees, grass, sunlight
Hilary M.	gift soap
Bethany M.	old skin
Jennifer K.	wool, cotton, anything yellow, anything
Cody R.	cuttlefish, handshakes, eyeteeth
Dylan H.	the mere mention of hornets
Brandon L.	foam pillows, roach motels
Susan W.	Indians, music, Indian Music
Lauren B.	twice sealed letters
Grace J.	candles, perfume, party sounds over water

Birthday Girl With Possum

No one wants to come
too near.   It's wild,
might climb out of her
arms, with its claws like
loops of gray icing. She
stares up at us, animals
poised to bellow. What
don't we want.

THE INTERRIBLE
Poem for what cannot be terrorized

It isn't people — we fall too much like houses —
& so it isn't houses, either.   But chimneys,
yes, the chimneys remain, sometimes a forest
of them, leaning sunward, saying to the basement,
That was close, & the basement echoes, *Close.*

    It isn't a wall, not a whole wall, anyway,
but somehow all the writing on the wall: every
Viva, every *Cuando,* every *Come home, Tommy,*
we need you.

    It's not the shroud, the shield, or helmet;
it's not the patch, the pole, or flag — no matter how
bad we want it, it's not the flag — but the T-shirt,
the low flying T-shirt.

                Not the skull, peeled skull,
but a picture of the skull, on the T-shirt, the helmet,
the wall. All pictures of the skull go on skulling.

Not the hand, the bottle, or the stone. Not the arrow,
the bullet, the rocket, but one tied shoe, at the curb
that was a step before a wall that was a house
with a chimney.

The chimney says, *Need you*. The wall

says, *Here*. The basement says, *Close*. The shoe says,

Only a road,   *only a road is not afraid.*

It's not the road. But the ground under every road,

the ground that stays alive because it's back is turned

& has been since we scared it.

A Thousand Chandeliers O.B.O.

A grape fell out of my mouth
looking up at your Empire
State Building costume

What windows were your eyes
behind, your mouth   I could barely
hear you over the tourists

waving from your observation deck
Nobody recognized my Tower
of Babylon hoop dress, but

people said it was pretty   One girl –
the Bank of China in Hong Kong –
said at least I didn't cram it down

everyone's throat like the World
Trade Center husband & wife
I don't think they could see thru

their masks; they just stood there,
not talking, not touching
their champagne   You gotta' feel

bad when people blow it like that,
how's anyone supposed to know
when it's safe to laugh at God

again   Is it true you went home
with the Duomo di Milano
He was hittin' the Jäger pretty early

I hope you drove   I got a cab before
the real partying started   It's still
hard for me to watch that kind

of drinking   Takes me back
to when I went for ages without
bathing or remembering who I loved,

when I slept where I fell

In The City of the Doll People

we came to record their quaintness

instead the sand was black,
the flowers were grey
instead the trees grew down into the earth,
so the roots piled, burned
instead the shrines were made from lifeboats,
we couldn't read the names
our guide was a local shaman, wherever
he lead us, people followed with food; pale fruit,
blue bread, a drink brewed from insects

instead we woke alone
the recorders got nothing
the pictures were blank, negative
after negative of flawless white;
even the well had vanished, the hole
healed over in the night
our clothes were taken, instead our bags were filled
with grass dolls, every man had five,
the women twelve or more

no one argued
instead we drank the last of the kerosene
then watched the desert for ships

BLACKBOARD JUNGLE

I don't linger in the teacher's lounge. My mail,
is there, as are the coffee & copy machines,
but when I'm done with them, I go. Something
about the place scares me, as though it's this room,
not my classroom, where I am most likely to be
exposed as a fake.
              I'm waiting on copies of Lowell's
turtle poems when a math teacher walks in & declares
animal crackers send *the wrong message* to children
because they imply all animals taste alike. Don't I agree
this could discourage them from trying new things?
A camel tastes nothing like a monkey, he yells above
the noise, *They're two totally different flavors!*
I want to ask how he knows this. I want to ask
what he means by *new things*, but frankly, I'm afraid.
He turns to the coffee maker & keeps shouting; I don't
catch the rest. It's sounds like *And I love that
sweet thang you doo!*
              Being noticed
freaks me out enough, now the Math Department
is hitting on me. But no, I can't have heard right.
What did you say? He opens a multitude of sugar
packets over his cup & repeats, *A lion is nothing
like a kangaroo.*
              I want to say nothing
is like a kangaroo. Captain James Cook brought
the word back from Australia in 1770 after his ship
ran aground on Queensland. There he met a local tribe
of aborigines & asked them about the giant, hopping
mice he'd witnessed; animals with massive legs
who carried their young in pouches like tobacco.
The chief replied *kang uru.*
              Cook tried a variety
of spellings in his journal; no doubt he said it aloud,
perhaps slowly to match it with the creature's
movements. Samuel Johnson later praised the word

as poetic, a perfect embodiment of the animal,
emphasizing his point by acting like one
in front of company. Dr. Johnson, a huge,
gravely featured man is said to have gathered
the tails of his coat into a pouch, & hopped about
the dining room, thick hands flapping before him,
as he chanted *Kangaroo, Kangarooo!*
                                    His guests
just stared, as the natives must have when Cook
repeated the word to them. Many now argue
it isn't a name but a whole sentence.
The chief was asking *What did you say?*
                                    It's not
a quiet debate. Cook never got the name of the tribe;
there's no way to trace the dialect. This second
linguists are fighting with historians, teachers
with students, experts of all kinds are raising
their voices, beating on tables, slamming doors
on each other because the whole thing is utterly
ridiculous. These were great men & great men
are always painted as fools over time. It's ego,
jealousy, an idiot's concept
                            of a concept.
My copies are done, the machine groans down.
Everything, says the math teacher, *everything
was meant to be eaten by something else. Ever
been to the Philippines?* I haven't, but Luzon,
the largest island, also means *What did you say?*
Yucatan is *I don't understand you.* The llama
comes form *Como se llama?* Indri, the short-
tailed lemur of Madagascar, means simply
look.

     Math is still gibbering at me, some crazy
patois I no longer follow. I take my stack of poems
in my mouth, shake my head at him & snarl
until he backs away, until he can't put me into
words. The room is mine, I leap out the door.

Bar Code Lullaby

Few words are lovely   as bar code
Little cage of snow,   crayon zebra
Wish you were here,   *Piet Mondrian*
Bar code & bar code   & bar code anon
To have a window on every book, every bottle,
a match-box smile   Toothy, ruthless, truthing
the cost of living   The shortest distance
between enemy lines   is a straight face
Hard road, car load,   tar toad dripping
from the curtain rod   A perfect mess
Cigarette fence, *burn*   *this town to the groun'*
Oh-say-some-more   please, say we'll get used
to these inches,   to the swipe of a stripe
of a white tiger   crouched on a number
we are too,   too dazzled to count

THE RENDERER

We just call it The House;
Slaughter makes people
uneasy. I've been there
a while now, throwing
bolts into bulls' heads,
into their frontal lobes
so they don't feel the rest
of it. Then a machine takes
their feet & the conveyor
moves'em on to the guys
who do the big cutting. I
could never do that part,
the disassembling. My job
is mercy. As each one
comes & I throw my bolt,
I try to think of something
nice, just in case they can
read me in that moment
when I open them. I tap
the trigger on my gizmo
& say aloud *pasture*, tap,
meadow, tap, *sweet grass*,
tap. But days are longer
than my imagination, I tend
to run out of things I know
they'd like, so I switch
to my own heart & say
woman, tap, *money*, tap,
house with a porch swing.

Lapsed Siren

When night has faded to its blond roots
and the moon fallen behind the bed of the sea
I come home,

                        dragging my fishnets,
my stolen coat, to sleep
beneath the stove.

                            It's warm there—
though the floor stays cool—and smells
like my mother's stove, the white Tappan
with its Porcelain and sweet grime,
its two little portholes

                        like a baby submarine,
like a merman's eyes.

For nine hours I'm a lost question mark.
When I wake the sun heads for the hills.
I find water in a dish that once belonged
to a blue-eyed cat, but Nimo is dead two years
and the dish is for me.

                        I've learned to fill it
before I leave, which is in another hour.
First must come a blouse, a pearl comb,
and a song sighed chorus to chorus,
Yo ho, Yo ho.

                  Then I go,
one hand to my chest, to the button
with the anchor on its face,

                      the other
          to my starboard pocket
where I touch the sand.

THE CLOD

Digging coal is like borrowing
from your girlfriend. She knows
it isn't coming back. Hell, she's
happy to help, if it keeps you
pleasant. But the earth is a girl,
not a woman. She'll trust you
with her dust while you waste it
in front of her. She's unwise,
ought to be hurt a lot sooner,
but you come back deeper, touch
more of her darkness, bring her
canaries. Funny how you never
see the birds die. You're into her
like always, but she's quieter.
So quiet, you finally notice
you haven't heard any singing
in a long time. She's already
closing, she closes fast. You
get out, though, usually. Learn
nothing, but how to start again,
elsewhere. She learns even less;
to go on, to die as a mine dies,
a man at a time.

TRAINING BRA

How soon can I trust them to go to town
without me,
             to know the cigarettes I like,
what streets to pass, what doors, to come
back with my dress in a pillow case

When I'm gray & drinking away my teeth,
will they wait outside the bar 'til I'm dark,

lead me home to bed while I insult them
And in the morning, the delible morning
of the old, will they remind me to eat
I don't think so
             They're no more teachable
than milk or sadness

ON SEARCHING FOR DYKES
Cento culled from forty-five voices on the internet

A flood bank is a high earthen wall that restrains water /
My sister is / a flood bank / My daughter is one / My mom /
my neighbor / my wife / is a flood bank / you can always tell
they're / flood banks / 'cause they got no breasts / because
they look run over / they go down /

Flood banks are often surrounded by clay / by magma / white
mica / they can have sunburns or freckles / If they have long hair,
it's in a ponytail / they have stupid haircuts / segmented
geometries, flood banks always have / hoarse, deep voices / mud,
granite, wood / gruff Canadian accents / Sandbags /

Flood banks are everywhere / the whole exploration block / You
see them / wherever there are women / trying to look normal /
sometimes wearing a dress / flooded with drift / a little smile /
maybe not knowing what they are / in the lowlands / collecting
ground-water / branches / baby shoes / your girlfriend /

They can last centuries / keep their features / they deepen /
get more masculine / when they dance / though they
never totally look like dudes / some vanish all together /
You'd never know there were flood banks here / just a place
where the ground rises / a row of sycamore trees

NYCTOPHONIA
On the nature of sound in darkness

You drink your ladders / brush your chair /

from the window's cream / clouds cloud

into each other / bruise / pile to rummage /

for sail /

        Time to cash some sleep /

if you can / What gave you the ocean

you're alone / Glisten at the door / here

clearly / cats stalking the tall glass / wind in

the whistles / flock of burrs in an arrow /

Hard to sea /

        The ear draws to a close /

You stay a wake / turn your willow over /

& over / faint lyrics / aprint in your cheek

THE GRAND

The Women's powder room was so large
on some mornings deer could be seen drinking
from the sinks.

And I can still hear my parents whispering about
the janitor who went missing in the Men's lounge
and was never found.

Police, bell boys, and all two hundred mustached
chefs from the kitchens formed a dragnet, locking arms
and crossing the room like a comb of paper dolls.

After six days, the man's wife called off the search
because he was probably staying away on purpose.
He'd *wander home on his own*, she said.

There was a picture of her in *The Times*, taken
outside the door. My mother clipped it out
to pray over and I stared at it in spells

wondering at the woman's rolled sleeves, the swans
on her apron, the word MEN above her shoulder.
Our prayers are somewhere over Japan by now.

My father ran an elevator. Car number 717.
He met my mother in it when she came to see
about a job in the gift shop.

She didn't get the job - less than ten years
experience - but she got him. They were married
in one of the themed chapels, I don't know

which one, but knowing my mother it had to be
pink and packed with Cupids. A modest reception
was held in a corner of the ball room; the only night

they went dancing. The floors were rosewood
and went on for a mile in any direction, sweeping up
to walls painted gold. They danced

for hours, though they could barely see the band
at the far end of the room. Just before midnight, clouds
formed beneath the chandeliers and it began to rain.

My father carried his wife up eighty flights of marble
stairs to a bridal suite—a gift from his boss
—where they danced until the moon disappeared

behind the east wing. I was born in that wing
and lived there until I was seven. That year my father's car
came loose. He was bringing some newlyweds

to the top when the cable snapped like licorice.
A fireman said my father had a dozen lilies
under one arm. He must have been holding them

so the groom could carry his bride to their door.
We went to live with my aunt on her farm, twenty
miles from town. Even so, in summer you could see

the hotel, a row of baby teeth on the horizon.
The farm house was a bunch of connected shacks
compared to the Grand. Though bright

and papered with flowers in one room or angels
in another, I saw it as dark, stained
like the legs of a French poodle.

I shared a bed with a step-uncle who never removed
his blond toupee. While he slept I would blow on it softly
until it lifted like a sail, moonlight catching

in the strands. Once, I blew it off completely, then slept
and woke falling as the ranting man turned
the mattress for his fugitive hair. Somehow

I remember falling for a long time, as if the floor
were at the bottom of a deep shaft. Next day
we were asked to leave and not come back.

We lived many places after that, forgetting each one
as soon as we left it. Years later, holding
my mother's hand in the hospital, we shared

a vision of the farm, the brownness and the stairs,
down and out, through flies and the banging
of screen doors. Then I got her ring. And his.

Two hundred dollars in the gift shop of the Grand
and not worth it, she said, *Use them to catch
deer.* I'm not sure how she meant it.

Was I supposed to wear them and hold out my hand?
Has anybody ever caught beauty that way? Don't you
have to not need it? Don't you have to fall into it

or get lost looking for something else? There is a city
where the hotel used to be and I live there. I go
walking in a park that was the putting green

and once I found a gold cufflink in the grass.
I keep it with the rings and a piece of bathroom tile
and a huge, square ashtray with the word Grand on it.

Stacked together they make a place, not a shrine
but a building with rooms large enough to put
the wind to sleep and where people work

and stay up all night making lists or coffee or love.
I don't need to look at it. I look at television
or a book. I look out the window of a train,

into the mouth of a tunnel swallowing the light
of the world as if it were a pearl onion. It is.

SOLDIER BABY

        asleep in the cradle of your helmet,
your name is a toy necklace. I'm tagged too,
a watched bird; my songs are taken from me
by postmen. If they come back, they come back
creased.

Baby, there's a country where people speak
sand, where they toss coins into fountains
of fire & wish to be left alone. All day the land-
scape paints itself the wrong colors, tears out
the page, starts again.

When you get there, don't sit still, don't let it
draw your one-yard stare. March in circles, like
the great desert turtle of the sky. Homebody.
I wish you could ride him here & quit
your naked platoon.

HYENAS IN THE TEMPLES OF PLEASURE
For Lily Marker

III

Great feet. Spectacular teeth. Eyes
that are sideways to everyone
but God.

I sing and they laugh. I make them
partners and they dance. I feed them
my city's dead

and they linger.

II

Only their sleep disturbs me. When
they are not laughing
or killing

but piled ear and testicle in marble
corners, breathing a decibel below
the fountain's purl,

I am eaten alive.

I

Dawn the owls call themselves
to rest. Quickly, for nothing
fanged is slow,

my grey animals rise and flicker.
And together we go, each
barefoot thief

to steal water.

"The Sea is the Ghost of the World"

Or it is all night
    bled from the stars
or it is the yoke of the moon
or it is a map of nothing
or it is young wine
or it is younger bread
or it is the mass grave of desire
or it is the ash of sleep
or it is the print of God's head
    in his pillow
or it is God
or it is His purse
      His cloak
      His drawbridge rising

In The Houses of the Night

In this island are certain glow wormes that shine in the night,
as doe ours…but give a greater light, so much that when the men
of the Iland goe any journeys in the night, they beare some of these
wormes made fast about their feet and head…By the light of these
also, the women worke in their houses in the night.
—Gonzalo Fernández de Oviedo y Valdés (1478 -1557)

In the houses of the night there are children who sleep, disfigured
by twilight, whose bodies mimic the dark margin of the landscape,
whose shadows terrify the children beside them. There are some
brave enough to face the wall, who laugh in their dreams, who ride
in boats small as leaves in a tub. Smaller.

There are men who take baths while smoking, while watching
the door, while talking to women. There are some who bathe
in total darkness, who walk wet to their beds, who stare
like horses, their eyes rimless, dark as tree water. They do not
dream. They would not survive it.

In the houses of the night there are dogs who speak like men,
there are birds who sing songs with words to them, garden
after garden of moths who mourn each closed flower, who die
of grief. There are spiders who make wreaths to catch them.
There are worms that call us into the ground like neon signs.

There are roads that remember canals, roads where the tar never
hardened & the blacktop gives like muscle, where the street lamps
tremble with the idling of sunken cars. The ants have gone mad
in their palaces. There are roads flooded with the ebon wings
of drone kings, roads that blow themselves out.

In the houses of the night there are women who whisper in closets,
who argue with mirrors, who talk easily to men in bathtubs.
There are some who bathe standing at a sink, who do it again,
who wash their bodies away. They do their sleeping like work.
They dream as a favor.

ACKNOWLEDGMENTS

The author gratefully wishes to acknowledge those publications where some of these poems first appeared.

"The Favor of Your Company" and "A Thousand Chandeliers O.B.O" first appeared in *FIELD*, Oberlin College Press.

"Noct" first appeared in *PANK*.

"1981" first appeared in *Luvena*, University of Guadilajara Press.

"Poem Ending on a Line by the Department of Water and Power" first appeared in *Dante's Casino*, Cassowary Press.

"Look" first appeared in the Write Bloody anthology *The Last American Valentine*.

"The Translation," "Alibi & Goodnight," and "The Renderer" first appeared in *Crimewave*, ITWASADARKANDSTORMYNIGHT Press.

"Lecture on Albert Einstein" first appeared as "Elegy Theory" in *DUCTS*.

"The Inquisition" first appeared in *Radius*.

"Lecture on Emmett Till" first appeared in *The Pinch*.

"Something You Can Use" first appeared in *SpotLit*, Spot Write Literary Corp.

"'So God Will Know You'" first appeared in *RATTLE*, Rattle Foundation.

"Fall Memo" first appeared in *Santa Cruz Good Times*.

"Birthday Girl with Possum" and "In the Houses of the Night" first appeared in *Ninth Letter*, University of Illinois Urbana Champaign.

"Blackboard Jungle" first appeared in *Askew*.

About the Author

This is Brendan Constantine's second collection of poetry. His first book, *Letters To Guns*, was released in 2009 from Red Hen Press. His work has also appeared in *Field, Ploughshares, Rattle, The Los Angeles Review*, & *RUNES*, among other journals. Mr. Constantine teaches poetry at Loyola Marymount University Extension and the Windward School in west Los Angeles. In addition to this, he regularly conducts poetry workshops for hospitals, foster care centers, and with the Alzheimer's Poetry Project.

He lives in Hollywood, California.

NEW WRITE BLOODY BOOKS FOR 2011

Dear Future Boyfriend
Cristin O'Keefe Aptowicz's debut collection of poetry tackles
love and heartbreak with no-nonsense honesty and wit.

38 Bar Blues
C. R. Avery's second book, loaded with bar-stool musicality and brass-knuckle poetry.

Workin' Mime to Five
Dick Richard's is a fired cruise ship pantomimist. You too can learn
his secret, creative pantomime moves. Humor by Derrick Brown.

Reasons to Leave the Slaughter
Ben Clark's book of poetry revels in youthful discovery from the heartland
and the balance between beauty and brutality.

Yesterday Won't Goodbye
Boston gutter punk Brian Ellis releases his second book of poetry,
filled with unbridled energy and vitality.

Write About an Empty Birdcage
Debut collection of poetry from Elaina M. Ellis that flirts with loss,
reveres appetite, and unzips identity.

These Are the Breaks
Essays from one of hip-hops deftest public intellectuals, Idris Goodwin

Bring Down the Chandeliers
Tara Hardy, a working-class queer survivor of incest, turns sex,
trauma and forgiveness inside out in this collection of new poems.

The Feather Room
Anis Mojgani's second collection of poetry explores storytelling and
poetic form while traveling farther down the path of magic realism.

Love in a Time of Robot Apocalypse
Latino-American poet David Perez releases his first book
of incisive, arresting, and end-of-the-world-as-we-know-it poetry.

The New Clean
Jon Sands' poetry redefines what it means to laugh, cry, mop it up and start again.

Sunset at the Temple of Olives
Paul Suntup's unforgettable voice merges subversive surrealism
and vivid grief in this debut collection of poetry.

Gentleman Practice
Righteous Babe Records artist and 3-time International Poetry Champ
Buddy Wakefield spins a nonfiction tale of a relay race to the light.

How to Seduce a White Boy in Ten Easy Steps
Debut collection for feminist, biracial poet Laura Yes Yes
dazzles with its explorations into the politics and metaphysics of identity.

Hot Teen Slut
Cristin O'Keefe Aptowicz's second book recounts stories of
a virgin poet who spent a year writing for the porn business.

Working Class Represent
A young poet humorously balances an office job with the life
of a touring performance poet in Cristin O'Keefe Aptowicz's third book of poetry

Oh, Terrible Youth
Cristin O'Keefe Aptowicz's plump collection commiserates and celebrates
all the wonder, terror, banality and comedy that is the long journey to adulthood.

OTHER WRITE BLOODY BOOKS (2003 - 2010)

Great Balls of Flowers (2009)
Steve Abee's poetry is accessible, insightful, hilarious, compelling,
upsetting, and inspiring. TNB Book of the Year.

Everything Is Everything (2010)
The latest collection from poet Cristin O'Keefe Aptowicz,
filled with crack squirrels, fat presidents, and el Chupacabra.

Catacomb Confetti (2010)
Inspired by nameless Parisian skulls in the catacombs of France,
Catacomb Confetti assures Joshua Boyd's poetic immortality.

Born in the Year of the Butterfly Knife (2004)
The Derrick Brown poetry collection that birthed Write Bloody Publishing.
Sincere, twisted, and violently romantic.

I Love You Is Back (2006)
A poetry collection by Derrick Brown.
"One moment tender, funny, or romantic, the next, visceral, ironic,
and revelatory—Here is the full chaos of life." (Janet Fitch, *White Oleander*)

Scandalabra (2009)
Former paratrooper Derrick Brown releases a stunning collection of poems written
at sea and in Nashville, TN. About.com's book of the year for poetry

Don't Smell the Floss (2009)
Award-winning writer Matty Byloos' first book of bizarre, absurd, and deliciously
perverse short stories puts your drunk uncle to shame.

The Bones Below (2010)
National Slam Champion Sierra DeMulder performs and teaches
with the release of her first book of hard-hitting, haunting poetry.

The Constant Velocity of Trains (2008)
The brain's left and right hemispheres collide in Lea Deschenes' Pushcart-Nominated
book of poetry about physics, relationships, and life's balancing acts.

Heavy Lead Birdsong (2008)
Award-winning academic poet Ryler Dustin releases his most
definitive collection of surreal love poetry.

Uncontrolled Experiments in Freedom (2008)
Boston underground art scene fixture Brian Ellis
becomes one of America's foremost narrative poetry performers.

Ceremony for the Choking Ghost (2010)
Slam legend Karen Finneyfrock's second book of poems ventures
into the humor and madness that surrounds familial loss.

Pole Dancing to Gospel Hymns (2008)
Andrea Gibson, a queer, award-winning poet who tours with Ani DiFranco,
releases a book of haunting, bold, nothing-but-the-truth ma'am poetry.

City of Insomnia (2008)
Victor D. Infante's noir-like exploration of unsentimental truth and poetic exorcism.

The Last Time as We Are (2009)
A new collection of poems from Taylor Mali, the author
of "What Teachers Make," the most forwarded poem in the world.

In Search of Midnight: the Mike Mcgee Handbook of Awesome (2009)
Slam's geek champion/class clown Mike McGee on his search for midnight
through hilarious prose, poetry, anecdotes, and how-to lists.

Over the Anvil We Stretch (2008)
2-time poetry slam champ Anis Mojgani's first collection: a Pushcart-Nominated
batch of backwood poetics, Southern myth, and rich imagery.

Animal Ballistics (2009)
Trading addiction and grief for empowerment and humor with her poetry,
Sarah Morgan does it best.

Rise of the Trust Fall (2010)
Award-winning feminist poet Mindy Nettifee
releases her second book of funny, daring, gorgeous, accessible poems.

No More Poems About the Moon (2008)
A pixilated, poetic and joyful view of a hyper-sexualized,
wholeheartedly confused, weird, and wild America with Michael Roberts.

Miles of Hallelujah (2010)
Slam poet/pop-culture enthusiast Rob "Ratpack Slim" Sturma
shows first collection of quirky, fantastic, romantic poetry.

Spiking the Sucker Punch (2009)
Nerd heartthrob, award-winning artist and performance poet,
Robbie Q. Telfer stabs your sensitive parts with his wit-dagger.

Racing Hummingbirds (2010)
Poet/performer Jeanann Verlee releases an award-winning book
of expertly crafted, startlingly honest, skin-kicking poems.

Live for a Living (2007)
Acclaimed performance poet Buddy Wakefield releases his second collection
about healing and charging into life face first.

WRITE BLOODY ANTHOLOGIES

The Elephant Engine High Dive Revival (2009)
Our largest tour anthology ever! Features unpublished work by
Buddy Wakefield, Derrick Brown, Anis Mojgani and Shira Erlichman!

The Good Things About America (2009)
American poets team up with illustrators to recognize the beauty and wonder in our
nation. Various authors. Edited by Kevin Staniec and Derrick Brown

Junkyard Ghost Revival (2008)
Tour anthology of poets, teaming up for a journey of the US in a small van.
Heart-charging, socially active verse.

The Last American Valentine:
Illustrated Poems To Seduce And Destroy (2008)
Acclaimed authors including Jack Hirschman, Beau Sia, Jeffrey McDaniel,
Michael McClure, Mindy Nettifee and more. 24 authors and 12 illustrators
team up for a collection of non-sappy love poetry. Edited by Derrick Brown

Learn Then Burn (2010)
Exciting classroom-ready anthology for introducing new writers
to the powerful world of poetry. Edited by Tim Stafford and Derrick Brown.

Learn Then Burn Teacher's Manual (2010)
Turn key classroom-safe guide Tim Stafford and Molly Meacham
to accompany *Learn Then Burn*: A modern poetry anthology for the classroom.

WWW.WRITEBLOODY.COM

WRITEBLOODY
QUALITY AMERICAN BOOKS

PULL YOUR BOOKS UP
BY THEIR BOOTSTRAPS

Write Bloody Publishing distributes and promotes great books of fiction, poetry and art every year. We are an independent press dedicated to quality literature and book design, with an office in Long Beach, CA.

Our employees are authors and artists so we call ourselves a family. Our design team comes from all over America: modern painters, photographers and rock album designers create book covers we're proud to be judged by.

We publish and promote 8-12 tour-savvy authors per year. We are grass-roots, D.I.Y., bootstrap believers. Pull up a good book and join the family. Support independent authors, artists and presses.

Visit us online:

WRITEBLOODY.COM

CPSIA information can be obtained at www.ICGtesting.com
Printed in the USA
BVOW05s0748120514

352963BV00001B/2/P